GOD, GIVE ME STRENGTH!!

By Pearl Lilly

GOD, GIVE ME STRENGTH!!

Copyright © 2013 Pearl Lilly

All rights reserved.

ISBN-13: 978-1481948449

pearllilly06@yahoo.com

Dedication

I dedicate this book to my aunt Annie Mae Lilly, who have always been there for me by supporting me, telling me stories, braiding my hair, cooking all of those delicious home cooking, spending time with me, but most of all....**for loving me!!!!!**

As a child, I had always thought that God had put me here to suffer, but my aunt had always told me that God had a better plan in store for me. Straighten up and Fly!!!!

My aunt Annie, my mother...I LOVE YOU.....

CONTENTS:

Chapter 11: Continues......　　Pg. 20

Chapter 12: The Home for Abused and Neglect Children.　　Pg. 25

Chapter 13: Helping out at the Home...　　Pg. 48

Chapter 14: Another Court Date!!!　　Pg. 69

Chapter 15: Living with my Grandparents in Alligator, Mississippi　　Pg.115

Chapter 16: Reunited with my Mother and brothers.....　　Pg.128

Chapter 17: Aunt Connie is coming....　　Pg.146

Chapter 18: My Stepfather is back!!　　Pg.155

Prologue

Through the grace of God and her Aunt Annie Mae Lilly; Pearl was able to use the strength and her courage to get through the events that was ahead of her. After being taken away to the home for Abused and Neglect, she had no idea what new challenge she would soon be faced with……

Book 2:

Chapter 11: Continues............

It was really difficult to talk about what I was going through. I wasn't even sure if I could trust her. I sat there quietly in her car until we reached her job. I wasn't sure if I should say anything to anyone. I was afraid of everything and everyone. Once we arrived at her office, I was told that I could get out of the car. The woman held my hand as we entered into her office.

I looked around and all I saw was a lot of old brown wooden chairs that were all lined up along both sides of the waiting room. The lady had asked me to sit in the first chair. She told me that she would be back to get me. A few minutes passed and the lady returned and asked me to come with her to the back of the office. We walked through a tall metal door. It was like every step that I took had grown longer and longer until we reached an office where another African-American lady had been waiting for us.

And Then…

Notes

Notes

Chapter 12: The Home for Abused and Neglect Children.

The thought of what my stepfather would do to me had always been on my mind, not knowing what he would do to my mother, my brothers, or my grandparents. But the most important thought was that, I didn't have to deal with him and longer but I wasn't sure if it was real or not. Boy, now that I was in a safe place, now that the secret was out, and the social workers here knew what had happened to me; I didn't have to worry about him coming to the home because they were there to protect me.

I didn't recall saying anything to the caseworker while she was driving me to the home for children. I just sat there in that warm heated seat of her car, thinking to myself, "What if I don't see my mother and brothers again"? I have to admit, I had started to regret what I had done.

I thought that maybe the social worker would just take me to my mother and asked her to leave my stepfather and that my brothers and I would be free from all of the abuse that we had suffered from him. But that never happen! The drive to the home for children seem like a forever journey to the unknown.

We drove up to a big brown brick building that had a big sign on the front of it say "Mississippi Home for Children", where the social worker had asked me to grab my back pack and let myself out of the car. The thought of feeling all alone, had crossed my mind and for that moment in my heart; I wanted to cry out for going back home, in Glen Allen. Mississippi.

Not realizing that the way to the home would change my life forever. After getting out of the car, I walked closed to the social worker as we approach the door of the home. The social worker ranged the door bell and this tall African American woman open the door and told us to come in. She had introduced herself to me as being Mrs. Florence and then to the other staff at the home. After that, she had taken me to my bedroom, where I had shared with four other children. Once I had put my things on the bed that was labeled with my first name, I was asked to come back to the staff's office with the social worker.

Mrs. Florence notice how sad I was as the social worker was getting ready to leave the home for her office. The social worker had stated to me that she would see me on Monday, because she wasn't going to be there in two days, then I had become a little angry because it was only Wednesday and I was so afraid of being there.

Mrs. Florence stated that, "I would be ok and the social worker would be back soon." Her office wasn't that far away from the home for abused and neglect children there in Greenville, Mississippi. I felt a little safer and better after the staff had told me that. At least, she wasn't that far from me and that if I needed her, the workers at the home would contact her. The most important thing that they were concerned about was for my safety and that I wouldn't harm myself.

After the social worker was gone, I recall telling Mrs. Florence that I was ready and that I would do what I'm supposed to while at the home and then she hugged me and took me back to my bedroom.

Mrs. Florence had want me to follow her as she had lead me into a dark empty room, that we all had to go in to see what our chores and the rules were at the home. Then asked to read the rules that were posted on the wall on the left side so that I was aware of what was expected of me and then I had to sign that I read and understood the rules. She then had taken me back to the bedroom and stated that I would share this bedroom with the other four kids and their names were Dawn, Judy, Sammy, and Tracey.

I found myself sitting next to Dawn and then we decided that I would sleep in the bed that was nest to her. Dawn was had to get ready to go back to the junior high school where Dawn had run track for them. The staff had stated that I would start on Monday.

Dawn had told me that she would be back in a few hours and that I should smile because she thought that I was I a safe place and that no one could hurt any of the kids there. I felt a little better after that and told her that I would see her soon.

Once all of my things were put away, I had gone the bathroom. Mrs. Florence then took me around to the other side of the home to how me the younger children and the rest of the home. Mrs. Florence stated that, If anyone would be in the living room, then we could only watch one movie and if we were going to watch regular television", because it had to be on one channel that everyone had agreed upon.

By the time we went all around the home dealing with all of the rules, it was time for the children to be walking in. Mrs. Florence stated that there were about a total of 14 children and they were all ages from 8 weeks old to 17 years old. I thought that because I was new at the home, and then I didn't have to do anything; but I was wrong, because the work that I pulled out from a big brown box would start at that moment.

I had chosen to wash the dishes and help with dinner. Mrs. Florence had asked me to go wash my hands and help with cutting potatoes and peeling the skin off of the apples and oranges. When Dawn returned from her track meeting, then she would help me with the dinner preparation.

After finishing with dinner, Mrs. Florence asked that everyone be silent for a moment. She wanted the children to meet me. I recall being so nervous about it. Mrs. Florence asked me to stand up and tell the other children my name. I stood nervously, and stated that my name was Pearl and I was from Michigan. A lot of the children, well at least the ones that were old enough to know what states were, didn't understand what or where Michigan was.

Then I had gone on to explain to them how I got to the home and that I lived in a small town called Glen Allen. Some of the children at the home knew what I was talking about and they knew that I didn't like being there at the home, but I had nowhere else to go to be safe.

After I was done telling the children about myself and where I was from, some of the children at the home had started to look at me sort of crazy. I just recall standing there looking really afraid, because I didn't think that the children at the home cared for me. Thinking that if I could just sit down, just maybe all of the attention would be off of me.

After standing thee for a few moments, Mrs. Florence had thanked me for introducing myself to the other children. Then she asked that each children to introduce themselves to me and tell a little something about themselves. Then other children stood up and introduce themselves to me. As the last child stood up to tell me her name, I thought to myself that I would be ok and that I had nothing to worry about.

I felt a little relieve, even though the thoughts of my mother and my brothers were a constant thought of great concerns. I didn't know what was going on down in Glen Allen. Was my mother looking for me and was she sad that I had not come home after school with my brothers.

I had gotten through with supper and the introduction of all of the children that were at the home at the time. I along with the other children was asked if we had wanted to watch television or play some board games. Whatever I had felt or thought about, I just knew that I had finally felt comfortable being at the home and that I was in a safe place. I said to Mrs.

Florence, "Thank you for helping me to feel safe and comfortable here at the home".

I just recalled her giving me this great big hug and can't really recall the emotion that had come over me. It had been so long since I ever knew what at safe hug had felt like! For one moment, I wasn't sure why, but I had started to think about all of the time my stepfather had told me that no one would care or love me the way that he had and I knew that the kind of love that he was giving to me was totally wrong.

It wasn't love at all, it was control and deceit! I stood there in the same spot for a moment, reflecting on everything that I had been going through and know I had a chance to be safe, I just wanted that for my brothers and my mother. I want them so bad that my heart aches.

My heart had started to hurt. I tuned towards the bedroom that I was in and went to lie down and cried myself to sleep. After sleeping for a while, I was time to get up and then another worker had told me that I needed to come out of the bedroom and interact with the other children. She held my hand and told me that I would be ok and that her name was Mrs. Carol. That she was there for the evening until the morning staff had returned.

Living in the home, I thought that I was a loser and that I had ruined my family. My life would never be the same; God would make me pay for telling what my stepfather had done to me. I had thought to myself that it would never be the same again and that there was no turning back. The thought that I would never see my family again had become too overwhelming for me. As I had gotten up out of the bed, I went into the bathroom to wash my face and brush my teeth.

I walked into the living room where all of the children were either watching television or playing some board games. As I approached the big red worn out sofa; became startled from a loud noise that had come from the kitchen.

Not realizing that there were any potential threat of a parent or other adults that would come to the home to see or get their child because they had miss them, it turned out that it was Dawn. She had picked up one of the kitchen table chairs and had thrown it at the kitchen window in order to break it so that she could get out and runway.

The staff had told all of the children to stay in their spot until they were able to get things under control. I just stood there thinking that I had made a big mistake of running my mouth to these peoples and maybe this place wasn't a good place any more. Because if it was, then why would any one of the children trying to break a window and get free from this place. Once the staff had got control of the situation, they took Dawn to the office and contacted her social worker.

I admit that I was so afraid and I did not want to stay there any longer. I just wanted my mom to come and get me from there. Al of the children were told to come into the kitchen, where the staff explained to us that, "Dawn had a bad visit from her mother and that she would be alright once she talked with her social worker".

I recall myself looking down at the floor because I so afraid and that I were really scared. I had a lot of thoughts running through my mind and that I didn't anticipating that it would be like that at the home. The staff reassured all of the children as well as for me that everything was ok and that we were going to continue with our daily schedule. I just sat there in the living room continued to watch television. I just blocked everything that had taken place out of my mind.

It was time for all of the older kids to meet with the staff to discuss what we were going through at school or within our emotion. We all expressed something that was either bothering us or something that we had wanted to suggest for example, one of the girls suggested that we have movie night on every Friday and another boy had stated that maybe we all could go shopping or to the skating rink.

The staff had responded really quickly to him. The answer to that was "NO!", because going to places like that would put all of the children at risk and there were children there order by the court to keep them safe from being kidnapped or even killed. They suffered so much abuse from their parents or other individual that were to help keep them safe, just like my stepfather was supposed to have kept my brothers and I safe from others; but we were looking for someone to help us stay safe from him!

I didn't know what to think. I just went on thinking that the hurt that we all experience in some form or another, didn't make it easier once we were removed from those horrible situation. I just kept on thinking and asking the staff as well as Mrs. Florence once she had return back to work, "Who was going to take care of them and me?"

That was all I wanted to know because I was so afraid of what would happen to us if we would have ever returned back home to our families.

A lot of my emotion had arouse from the thought that Mrs. Florence and the others had believe in me and there were times that I thought maybe it was all just in my head. All I knew was that I just wanted to go back home to my mother and help her take care of my brothers and keep all of them safe! That was all I had wanted.

Notes

Notes

Chapter 13: Helping out at the Home....

There at the home for abused and neglected children, there was this little baby that was there because he had been abused by his mother. I believe that this little baby, a boy; was probably around eight or nine months old when he arrived at the home. The little baby was an African American child and that he was not originally from Greenville, Mississippi. His family had moved there from the east coast, not sure which state but not from there.

The little boy baby looked really strange. His face was really old and wrinkled looking and that it had appeared as if someone had glued his skin back to his face. One of the staff members has stated that the little boy had looked that way due to the abuse that he had suffered from the hand of his own mother.

The mother was on drugs and that one night she was using really bad, the little boy had started crying a lot and too much; when he wouldn't stop crying, his mother grabbed him and put him in the bath not realizing that the water was too hot, she put him in the tub and the baby was burned really bad.

The hot water was up to high one of the workers had stated. But regardless, it was the hands of the mother that caused those injuries to the baby. The worker had told us, that we couldn't say anything about the baby's injuries or why he was there. I didn't see or observe any other bruises or scares on the baby other than his face, but that was bad enough. Because he would have to deal with those horrible facial scares for the rest of his life.

I thought about my life and everything that I had gone through, thinking about the poor little baby and how much pain he must of have felt while being in that hot water. I thought about my own pain of my stepfather molesting an draping me every chance that he had, I knew how much pain I had suffered from, but I was older and I just couldn't imagine or even though about how I must have felt as a bay that age of the pain that I had dealt with.

Not realizing that it was late because I didn't really pay any attention to the time at that point in my life. It seem as if time had stopped on me, which made wanting my mother even difficult, but I was able to peak out of the living room window to only discover that it was dark outside. My mind had started to wonder, did my mom worry about me and did she even go to the school to look for me? Where was my mother? I had thought to myself over and over again until I felt myself get anxious and sick.

I approached the staff and asked if I could call my mother they had told me that I couldn't and that I could be ok while I was there. The staff had reassured me that my mother would come to visit when the court and the worker allowed her to but for now I needed to not worry about anything, just try to not think about anything but being a kid. The worker had told me and the other children at the home to go and wash our hands because it was time to eat dinner and then have a snack afterward.

I didn't want anything to eat; I just wanted my mother. The one of the staff just wanted me not to worry and that I needed to eat something to keep my strength up. So I just went into the bathroom to wash my hands and went into the dining room with everyone else so that I could eat and just go to the bed. After eating my dinner, I asked if I could go to bed.

The staff stated that it was time for all of the children to get ready for bed and that it was ok if I had excused myself before everyone else. I clear my place at the table and took my plate to the kitchen and then said thank you to the staff and went to the bedroom to get ready for bed. Once I was in the bedroom, I sat on the bed thinking that I was so stupid and now I wasn't going to see my mother and brother ever again.

I felt as if I was in some kind of prison and that here it was again, that I was being done wrong. The staff wouldn't let me leave or call my mother. What was I to do?

I went to take my shower and put on the night clothing that the social worker had bought for me and then got down on my knees and preyed like I never preyed before.

I want God to just listen to my heart and allow me to me to go back home with my mother and brothers. Please God, just hear me! As I got into bed, one of the staff members came and sat beside of me and told me that I just needed to stay there for a few days until they figure out what was going on with my case and them maybe the worker would allow me to go home to my family. I responded with a nod and told the staff worker ok and then lay down and cried myself asleep. I had started to hate myself at that very moment and the thought of wanting to die had taken over my mind. But I just laid there until I went to sleep.

The next morning, I had woken up and thought that my mother would come for me. So I got up and brushed my teeth and had gotten dress. I sat at the window waiting for my mother to arrive while I sat by the front door. That morning, Mrs. Florence had come back to the home to get some paper work that she had left that Friday before going home for the weekend. I ran to her and grabbed her legs, just screaming for her to take me home with her and then she could take me back to Glen Allen, Mississippi, so that I could be with my mother.

She stated that she couldn't and that I would be just fine. I just needed to calm down, so that I could just enjoy the time that I had while I was there.

"Don't worry Pearl!" she stated and then she left.

I became filled with anger and rage and I wanted to kill everybody that had ever hurt me, because if they wouldn't have abuse me by having sex with me then I could have still been home with my brothers and my mother. I thought about each one of them and if I could have been old enough, then just for one moment I could have defended myself from them.

I wouldn't have ever had to be there at the home in the first place. I stormed in the bedroom as I approached the bed, I through myself on the floor. I recall screaming at the top of my lungs until the staff workers had come in to see what was going on with me.

"I WANT MY MOM!!" I screamed and scream…**"I WANT MY MOM, PLEASE!"**

Realizing that I was going to be there, I just told myself that I was stoke there and I should just get used to it. I decide that day, that I would just help out at the center and try to make the days go by faster because it was only Saturday and I still had that day as well Sunday left before the social worker would return back to the home to get me. But that wasn't the cause.

That following day, I had to follow all of the rules just like the other children at the home and complete all of the chores that were assigned to me. I After completing my chores, I waited patiently for the staff to tell me what I needed to do next, so I went back into the bedroom and laid down until they came to get me. It wasn't that I was tired, I was just missing my family and no matter what chores or activities that they had given me to do; my mind was still on them.

I That evening, the staff had told us that we needed to get our clothe ready for school for in the morning, but I didn't understand why I had to get my clothing ready because I was going back to my school in Glen Allen. But the staff had stated that I wasn't and I was going to start attending Greenville High School and that I wasn't going back to me to my old school. At the dinner table I couldn't eat anything; I became very bitter towards everyone.

Mrs. Florence had addressed the situation that I was having and redirect my behavior. I recall staying up a little longer than the other kids because my social worker was stopping by to bring me some school supplies.

I didn't care, I wasn't going and that was that! I went to bed after the worker had come and gone, Mrs. Florence had taken me to my bedroom and told me that I would be ok and that I just needed to calm down. "Everything would be alright, try not to worry so", she stated.

As I had gotten ready for bed, Mrs. Florence had given me a brand new pair of pajamas, I could even remember when the last time I sleep in a pair of children pajamas, because I had started to sleep in my clothes at night in order to keep my stepfather from molesting me and when I was brave enough, just then would I get my brothers and run away through all of those long rows of cotton fields, that high-grass un-kept grave yard, and runt down football field in order to get to that long paved road leaving out of Glen Allen, Mississippi.

I shared a bedroom with the other three girls and as Mrs. Florence had left the room for a few moment, Dawn got out of her bed and gave me a hug and told me that I would be ok and not to cry. Because when she first came to the home, she was so afraid and nervous. Dawn was 15 years old and she had been at the home for about eight months prior to my arrival and she felt ok there. The staff had treated her with kindness and so much care.

Dawn was really kind to me, right from the time that we had first met each other's. Dawn had been my friend from that point on; until it was time for me to leave the home when we all learned that my grandparents were coming for me. Dawn and I would remain friends for a long time and that we would support each other's, but that didn't happen because my grandparents were coming for me.

I remember the time that we would sit for hours during the night exchanging stories about our lives and the things that we had gone through. She had mention that she wasn't from Mississippi and that her family had come here from Texas, she just wanted to go back home to find her father. Her mother and her stepfather use to do abusive things against her and say that the "Devil was going to take her away". Dawn had continued to run away from her home so that she wouldn't have to suffer any longer.

Many nights Dawn and I had stayed up talking about what and how we wanted our lives to would be once we were out of the home for children. I had started to feel a little better after that and the thought of escaping from the home didn't seem like the main and only priority of mines. After talking about what we were going to do, Dawn went on talking about here boyfriend. I just remembered telling her that I was too young for all of that and the thought of even talking about a boyfriend would have gotten me and my family killed. I belonged to my stepfather and nothing or no one would ever change that. I needed to listen and did what he had told me to do in order to keep my mother and brothers safe. I had blocked ever boy or males out of my mind, with the exception of my brothers!

    After talking with Dawn about so many things that young girls `usually talk about, but for me; any subject regarding boys were off limits. I didn't want to discuss any more talk about boys, so I told Dawn that I just wanted to go to sleep and wait for my mother to come and pick me up. Dawn looked at me and shook her head and told me that it was going to happen like that. I would have to wait a long time before I would ever see my family again.

I lay there thinking, "What if she was lying to me or no?" I would just die if I couldn't see my family again. In my mind, I thought that there would be no need to live any longer! I couldn't shake the feeling of wanting to die. So I just closed my eyes and went to sleep so that I could wake up the next morning, with the hope of seeing my social worker and ask her could I see or even go back home to my mom.

As I remember laying there in the bed, it was so difficult turning my brain off. I just keep thinking and thinking, "What have I done?" I just hope that my mother didn't hate me!!!

The next morning, Dawn asked if I was ok and that I needed to get up and get ready for my social worker. She also had stated that she hoped that everything goes ok with my visit with the social worker and that she hopes that she would get a chance to see me before I left, if I was leaving today.

I hugged her and told that I had felt the same way and I hoped to see her as well.

Notes

Notes

Chapter 14: Another Court Date!!!

After I had gotten ready that morning, my social arrived at 10:00 that morning. She had taken me into the family room, where she sat with me to discuss what was going to take place that morning. I just wanted to know when and if I could just see my mother and brothers. The social worker had asked that I sit and listen to her. I respected her by calming down and listen.

The social worker went on to tell me, "that we had to go to court in a few days, then the judge would decide if I could go back home to mother". I wasn't sure what I was going to do when I had got to court. I just remember that I wanted to tell my mother what I want to tell her about what I was going through all of my life.

The thought that I would have to face my stepfather had become a routine. Those thoughts had ran through my mind ever since the social worker had mention the court date. The social worker reminded me that I had nothing to be afraid of, because they were going to be there to protect me and secondly; he would most likely not show up in the first place! The social worker had notified the home for children staff about the next court date and time so that they could prepare me ahead of time.

Going to court that day was only to see if my mother was going to comply with the states and the judge's order in order to get me back. My mother needed to get a home for us children where my stepfather couldn't be in the home. That also meant for me and my brothers that we would be back together again and that she had to get that evil man out of our lives!

I just wanted to be a family again and for all of us without home of course to move back home to Michigan where our families were. When the next court date had arrive, I wasn't afraid anymore of him, I knew that the dirty secret was out and that he could no longer harm me. Those days of him raping me several times a day was over and for the first time in my life, I could sleep in my bed without worrying what was going to happen at night. Now that we had gone to court, my mother needed to everything to keep me safe and that he could not be around.

As a kid, I really had a hard time adjusting to everything that was going on. I mean, my worker had made everything that was going on easy, but I did not understand why I couldn't go home that day. The court date had gone by like a shooting star. Things did not go as well at the court, I thought that I could go home with my mother at that point, but the judge did not allow me to go back with her.

So that meant that I had to go back to the home for children until my mother had done the things that the y had ordered her to do. I felt really bad and that I felt that my mother must have hated me for hurting her like that and tearing the family apart. I don't recall my mother looking or speaking to me during the court proceeding.

I thought that she was angry at me for everything that I had cause and that maybe she didn't want me back after that. After leaving the court room, that meant that I had to stay at the shelter until someone else in my family would come to get me. I felt as if I was a piece of meat or luggage that was left behind unclaimed.

I wasn't sure what was going on with the decision of the judge. I was told that my mother did not do what the Department of Family Services had asked of her and that meant that I had to wait e what was going to happen to me. He worker had stated that if no one would come for me, then I would continue to be "Ward of the State of Mississippi" then I would either age out of the system or be placed with another family.

I don't really recall how long it had taken for anyone in the family member would contact the department of Family Services to get me. I remember having a few visits from other peoples in the family but never my mom. I recall being really afraid that I would never see my mother again. I can only imagine that when small children are taken away from their mother, the pain that they must have felt. I was older; therefore it didn't hurt as much, because I understood that it was for my safety.

They only thing that I wondered was that I was afraid that no one would ever come for me. Maybe everyone hate me!! Then what would happen to me? Where would I live? I was an orphan of the state and that I could not go or do anything anymore I wouldn't see my mother and brother ever again. I had to prepare myself for that. At that moment in my life, I really felt alone in my life. Mo mother, no brothers, and most of all NO GOD!!

There were so many things going on in my mind that the thought of asking and begging God, to give me strength to continue living was like asking a wino for his last bottle. I knew that my patience was running out and I was tired. So at that point in my life was when I had started to store everything that I was thinking and feeling inside.

I couldn't trust anyone anymore!! At that point, I was alone, so from then on I would never tell a soul what my stepfather and all of those other monsters had done to me. I had in my mind, gone mad. I was very angry and hated everything and everyone around me. I told myself that I would talk or speak another word as long as I lived.

I had lost all faith in the social worker, judicial system, most of all GOD. I thought that if I had told the truth; then I wouldn't have to hurt any longer, but that was only the beginning. I lost my soul and the thought of dying became a major part in my life.

I thought about different ways that I would die. The easiest way was to just take a hand full of pills or stab myself with a butcher knife. It really didn't matter how, just as long as I had done it!

Living life without my brothers and mother was incomprehensible. Why was God doing this do me?

The thought of remaining in the children's home for a long time frame, as a kid was like forever and there wasn't a way that I would stay there that long until a family member would determine if I was good enough to care for. I t had taken a toll on me and my heart! I had to get out of the home, one way or another.

I waited for the days that had followed by my failed court date. I knew then, that there would be no way that I would ever leave the home, therefore, I had to put a plan in place. I had decided that when the staff at the home would take and drop me off at school, then I would run away and there weren't anything that they or the courts would do to me. I would be free and if I couldn't return back to my family then I wanted to be a lost soul in this world, or dead!

I remember making my plans to run away, but it seemed as if they had read my mind, because it was like I never had any time alone after that. It was as if the worker had known what I was planning to do and continued to pick me up every day after that. I had to be patience as if I was that mouse trying to find the right time to get the cheese of the mouse trap. Many days had gone past, when I had sat there at the home for days.

I remember that the worker had told me that she was going to let me attend school again, because all I had done was laid in the bed or sat alone on the corner. I didn't want to interact with anyone at all. The thought of being alone without my brothers and mother became a reality. I needed to prepare myself.

After a few days, I packed one of my back packs with a few clothing and personal needs items, and then waited until it was time for the social worker to take me to school. The next morning, I grabbed both my school bag and the packed one and went to the worker's car and sat quietly. I have to admit that I was really nervous, but mostly afraid. I was afraid that no one wanted me and that in my mind, my life was over! I inhaled as hard as I could to shake the fear and got the thought out of my mind of when and if anyone was coming to get me.

The angry little girl just didn't give a damn any longer. I build up the strength to run away and then, I just had to stay calm and keep myself together until she dropped me off. We arrive at the school, as I jumped out of the car, the worker grabbed my hands and told me that everything would be ok, just give her another chance to make contact with my grandparents.

Something in my heart believes her and that it messed everything that I was going to do, up. Should I believe her or just proceed with my plan of running away. In my mind, I thought that she was playing games with my mind and I couldn't handle that any disappointment again. If she was lying to me, then then I would fix her and everyone else. The only solution was death and that was that!!

I had decided that I would give the social worker a few more days and that was it! No More! In a few days, then hopefully the worker would hear something and for me that would be the best, even though I contemplated suicide, I was really afraid.

The thought that the worker was not going to find a family member that would want me and if she could that would be a blessing as well as wonderful news. A few days had gone past, no word at all and that was when I knew that everyone hated me and that I wasn't worth anything.

I remember that it had to have been on the fourth day, when the worker came to the school to pick me up and shared the news of my grandparents wanting to get me and that they were going to be there in Greenville, Mississippi in a few days. I remember tears running down my eyes and that my heart ached for joy.

The feelings of joy and every other emotions that overwhelmed my whole body and mind was amazing, every time I thought about it, I was in disbelief. I wouldn't have to stay at the home any longer. The staff and children at the home were very kind and respectful towards me, but I just want it my own family; those who really knew and cared for me. I knew that my grandparents would protect me and care for me.

I wouldn't have anything to worry about. As I waited for my grandparents to come, I recall that I had a lot of reservation regarding my grandparents. Not that they love move or would still come to get me from the home for children; it was that what if they had blamed me for breaking up my mother's home. Would they be mad at me or not; as a child, what was I supposed to have thought!

I waited for the day that my grandparents to arrive with anticipation and I think it was probably a few week that had went past before they had actually arrived in Greenville, Mississippi to get me. I was about around twelve or just a little close to thirteen, when my grandparents would come to get me out of the home.

I was no longer abandon! I recall that my grandfather had got out of his car and walked up to the home, but as he approached the door, one of the staffs at the home for children open the door and let my grandfather in. My grandfather hugged me and asked if I was alright, I replied, Yes Sir." A tear rolled down my face as I was consumed with so many emotions. I couldn't believe it, I was free and most of all, I was SAFE!!!

I remember getting all of my things and saying good-bye to all of the children especially Dawn, because I knew that I would never see them again and for Dawn, I hoped that her and I would eventually cross each other's pate someday. I miss her for who she was and how she kept me calm and safe while at the home. For the staff, I will always be grateful to them for everything that they had done for!

As I had taken my belonging to my grandfather's car, he reached out and gave me a knock on my head. I remember as a young child back home in Lansing, Michigan he had done that to all of us children as his gesture of hello. At first I was nervous and that I wasn't sure if they was happy to see me or if they felt as if they had an obligation since no one else wanted me. My grandmother gave me a great big ole hug and asked if I was ok. I replied, "Yes Mamm".

After putting all of my things in the car, I went to give everyone another final hug, and walked away. For just a brief moment, I felt sad. Being transferred from one place to another, it was really difficult for me. I stayed at the home for little over eight months and still no word if I was ever going back home to my mother. I felt lost and thrown away. My grandparents came for me and that was all that matter, I guess!

I wasn't sure where we were going, since I had never been anywhere else in Mississippi otter than Glen Allen, Myersville, Rolling Fork, and now Greenville. My grandparents didn't tell me where we were going, I just remember sitting in the back seat quiet as a mouse and just watching everything as we drove down that long hot dusty Mississippi Delta roads.

We had driven for such a long time; it was almost dark when we had arrived in this town to what I would discover to be Alligator, Mississippi. As I sat patiently awaiting the arrival of our final destination, my grandfather had made a right turn on this black pave road that lead us through an wooded area, then down a curvy roads that lead into a small town that appeared to have only about four to five small country General stores, small convenient gas station, laundry room, and post office which was just big enough to go in and out of it in order to collect or distribute going mail.

I recall looking kind of confused because this location was like some scene off of a Cold

Case television episode that was filmed in some parts of Mississippi that hung a lot of African-American peoples. I have to admit, that I was really scared and that didn't know what my grandfather was thinking, but we needed to get the Hell out of there!

After driving through the small town and down the curvy road, the car came to an abrupt stop. My grandparents had this fear in their face. I can't really recall what they were saying, but after the car stop, my grandfather yelled, "Be Quiet!"…

I asked him what was going on and he replied, "Be quiet child!"

As I sat quietly, I notice that my grandfather had reached under the blue leathered seat of his car to reach for his gun and pointed it out of the driver's window. It seemed as hours had gone past while we sat there waiting on whatever it was in the road. I was a noisy little thing s I have to admit, silence was killing me.

I leaned forward to see what was in the road and oh my God, it was an big ole' alligator lying in the middle of the road as we reached the turn to the right of another gravel dirt road to some trailer houses that we would eventually call home for some several months. They were lined up like a pack of trains awaiting pick up to carry whatever its content was.

As we allowed the alligator to cross the road completely, we proceeded to turn on the road and arrived at my grandfather's brother and wife house. I was afraid because I wasn't sure if I would have liked the place furthermore the peoples! We got of the car and went indie the house. Greeting us at the door was my grandfather's brother's sister-in-law Ruby.

Ruby had this strange look in her face as she did not want us there, but my grandmother as strong and assertive as she was, looked a Ruby and told the cow to get out of her way. She went to tell me that she hated that old bitty and that she had eyes on my grandfather. I looked at her and scrunched my eyes indicating that I had my grandmother's back and the that old bitty better not call herself messing with my grandmother and she better had gotten her eyeballs off of my grandfather!

As we got inside, we were greeted by my grandfather's brother and wife and they told us to "Come on in and make ourselves confront able". I had taken my place on the love seat that was closes to the door. My grandmother had sat down in the recliner, while my grandfather went to the kitchen with his brother.

I recall that right after my grandfather had left the room where we were sitting waiting patiently on what was going to take place after we had arrive in the small town of Alligator, Mississippi; to only discover that we were going to stay the night there. My grandmother had this red anger in her as if she was a raging bull. She looked at my grandfather as he returned to the room and said, "James, get your ass over here right now, I mean now!" My grandfather said, "Just for a little while, Please".

I became upset with myself, because my grandparents left Michigan to come all the way down to the south to care for me, which resulted with them becoming angry with each other's and I knew that it was my fault.

Time had gone bye as if we were already living there, not realizing that what would have been supposed to have been a short stay ended up being several long miserable months. My grandmother and I were not happy at all that my grandfather had taken us to live in Alligator, Mississippi instead of finding our own home.

My grandfather had told my grandmother and me to just deal with living there until he rented or bought a house for us. I felt as if I had no choice or say in the matter, just respect what my grandfather said and stay in my place, A Child!!!!

While living in Alligator, Mississippi there would many events and incidents that had taken place while living with my grandfather's brother's sister-in-laws house. Boy oh Boy was it ever!!! That was when I really learned that some elderlies can be a Bitch!!! Yes, a Bitch!! Excuse my French, but when you read more of the story; I promise you will say, "Hmmmm, B....!!!!

Ok, where do I start? Well, it was on a Monday morning, t was already hot and muggy. There were the sounds of birds chirping in the air. As the sun cast its hot beaming rays on the window of the bedroom where I laid quietly, due to nervousness; I got up ready for my day. Not really knowing what the day would bring me, I went to take a shower and to eat breakfast.

My grandmothers hate it when peoples lay around all day. Therefore, I knew that I needed to gone and get up before I was in trouble.

I finished putting on my clothes, went to brush my teeth, when I noticed in the other bedroom that there were a lot of old pictures. Pictures of family members that served in World War I and II; I recall these pictures being very interesting, but at the same time scary. They looked like they were looking right through me as if they knew what had happened to me and as if they were watching me like I was a common thief.

Every step that I had taken, their eyes had appeared to move in the same direction that

I had moved. I reached the bedroom door and walked as if I had fire set to my behind. I remember being so afraid and then, telling my grandmother that I hoped I never had to sleep in that room. I was so afraid! But not realizing that the old bitty was listening to our conversation. She stormed out of the room and told my grandfather that she didn't want anyone sleeping on the living room chair and that I either had to sleep in the bedroom or find somewhere else to sleep!

I just thought to myself, that she was an old ugly bitch and I hated that old lady. I was always taught to respect my elders, but she was a fucking monster!! There were other times that she had snitched on my grandmother and I because my grandmother waited for her to go to bed and then she would tell me to sleep on the chair.

I was deathly afraid of sleeping in the bedroom, with those big bugged eyed peoples in the old picture frame. But there was a time that I had no other choice but to sleep in the bedroom. It was about several days later when I was made to sleep in that bedroom and that I had nothing to say about it. I remember crying to my grandmother and that I felt like those pictures were looking and watching me.

I went to bed as I was told to and that I just remember laying there, still as a dead dog lying stiff on the side of a road after getting hit by a semi-truck. I couldn't breathe. My eyes rolled away slightly away from the pictures, in order to capture my thoughts. I prayed to God that night as I had done many nights before, but with hopes that he had heard me that time.

I prayed and I prayed. God, please find a way for my grandparents to get a home for us. I didn't want to be a bother to them. I thought to myself, I would have been better off if I just went ahead with running away or even killing myself! Then at least other peoples wouldn't have to suffer because of the mess that I had caused!

The next morning, my grandmother and grandfather had gone for a long drive through the country roads. I recall us driving past the old Parson Prison between Clarksdale and Greenwood, Mississippi. There were a lot of days we had done things out of the moment in order to stay out of the old lady's way. Soon time had come when that wasn't enough.

There were lots and lots of days that had come when we had arrived back to the house and some of our things were either missing, in the trash, or even cut up. Yes, cut up!

Wow...I could not believe nor understand what we had done to make this old lady so hateful towards us. She really targeted my grandmother. My grandmother had expensive things such as jewelry, wigs, bras, and clothing. This old woman would just cut away leaving my grandmother with rags!!!!

I was so damn angry for what that old bitty had done to my grandmother and I wanted to kill that damn woman. The anger turned into rage and that the best thing that had happen was that my grandfather needed to move us out of that woman's home and get us our own place to live.

There were a lot of days that my grandmother and I had packed up a small bag (for her gun), fishing tackle box, water cooler, and a medium size lunch box container that was packed with round bologna, water, Pepsi, vanilla wafers, and some other snacks that she had packed for us. My grandmother and I had put on our straw hats and heading down to the old fishing hole where we had caught a lot of bass, catfish, and even an small turtle. '

I have to admit, I was a little afraid, because the grass was always high and the thought of either alligators or snakes would have gotten us. My grandmother was never afraid, afraid of nothing or anyone!! She was a strong woman. I was name after my grandmother, but we called her "Madeal" short for Mother Dear. My grandfather was James, but we called him Daddy. He loved blues, jazz, and the soulful tunes of the Aquarius singing group. My grandmother was Baptist, while my grandfather was Jehovah Witness, what a combination....

As a little girl, my grandparents were the world to me!!

As my grandmother and I continued on our journey to the fishing hole, we didn't come across any alligator or snakes. I remember sitting down at the fishing holes for hours just to keep from going back to that old bitty's house. But as soon as we had arrived, we had discovered that there were other damages to our clothing's and or something had gone missing, like my grandmother's necklace that my grandfather had bought her. My grandmother just told me to sit still and be quit!

As I sat there, thoughts had gone through my mind as to what my grandmother was thinking about and what in God's name what she was about to do. I remember that as I was sitting there in that spot, my grandmother reached for her bag and walked into the other room where the sound of rattling was coming from.

My grandmother raised the bag that contained her gun inside of it, placing her right hand inside of it and enter into the room. There she was, that old bitch!! She was going through my grandmother's dresser drawer and cutting up her red beautiful church dress. There were pieces of cut up clothing items everywhere.

"What in the hell"! That was what my grandmother yelled out at the old bitty as she continued into the other room. My grandmother yelled out for me to go get my grandfather and tell him to get his "Ass in here!" I ran as fast as I could, to get myself from crying. Even though I hated that lady, I didn't want my grandmother to shot her and be taken away from me.

I felt a lot of anger towards myself, because my grandparents could have been in the comfort of their own home back home in Lansing, Michigan instead of being there to help care for me. At that moment I knew that my life and everyone around me would have been better if I was DEAD! Their lives would have been back to normal in my mind.

I continued to get my grandfather from the other house where he had sat throughout the day with his brother. Once I had approached the house, I yell for my grandfather and told him that the lady was at the house going through my grandmother's things and that my grandmother had taken out her gun. I was so scared that my grandmother was going to kill that lady.

My grandfather and the other men had jumped from their seats and ran toward the house. My grandfather's oldest brother told my grandfather to get my grandmother as he got his sister-in-law from the house.

My grandfather pleaded with my grandmother to put her gun back in her purse and that he had promised that he would get us our own home. My grandmother listed and put the gun away, then told my grandmother and I to go get in the car, so that we could leave.

After everything had calmed down, my grandfather had come to the car and we pulled off. I wasn't sure where he was taken us, because normally if would have taken a ride through the country roads, we would have gassed up the car and pack the back with lunch meat and vanilla wafers or crackers.

My grandfather had told my grandmother that he would put us in our own home and after some several hours had gone past, he met up with some tall white man. I eventually found out from another family member that the man was the same man that my grandparents with their children on the plantation down in Alligator, Mississippi. After my grandfather had spoken with the man, he gave my grandfather a set of key and then we left.

My grandfather returned back to the car and told my grandmother that everything would be ok and that he got us a place to live. My grandmothers shook her head nodding yes and then turn looking out of the car window. Everything was alright after that. My grandmother wasn't upset any longer and that after that day, as a child I remember the fear that was on my grandfather's face after my grandmother had pulled that gun out of her bag.

We returned back to the trailer house to get all of our things and headed up the old dirt gravel road heading out of the led plantation land. We didn't have that far to travel. We had approached the end of town the same spot that lead us there, crossing the highway heading in the same direction north about some 30 feet, turning left down another dirt graveled road then turning right to a house that looked homely, runt down shack.

The house stood in the middle of a big ole cotton-bean field. I just stood there shaking my head; I wasn't sure about this, because I had nothing to say about anything, I just needed to be a grateful child and kept my mouth shout! I gathered all of my things and got out of the car.

My grandmother watched my grandfather as he went in to open the door to the house and went in to check to see how the house was. Once he had gone in, he returned to share with us that the house was ok and that it looked real nice inside.

We went inside of the house and looked around and he was right, the house looked ok. There were beds in all of the bedrooms, furniture, dining table, and more. I sat and thought to myself, "How in the world did he get the house like that, that soon?"

My grandfather had shared with me that he had already gotten us a place to live, my grandmother just needed to be patient.

I was so amazed that he had already had everything together, but I was still till this day, how did he arrange all of that.

My grandfather was the best man that I have ever none and that no matter what he made things possible for us…

Notes

Notes

Chapter 15: Living with my Grandparents in Alligator, Mississippi

As a little girl, age 12, the longing for my mother was very difficult for me; but I knew that maybe someday that I would soon be reunited with my mother. In the meantime, I just remembered that I had my grandparents and that I had to do what I needed to do to survive.

Living with my grandparents I had a sense of safety and that I didn't have to worry about any old bitty trying to harm my grandmother or me. I felt like I could walk around the house and not worry about anyone watching or bother me. I could really just be a kid and play outside or anywhere that I wanted to.

There were so many days that my grandparents and I had walked around the house to see what the landscaping was like and that we had discovered an old slave house that had been there in Alligator, Mississippi ever since my grandfather was a little boy. My grandfather was born and raised down in Alligator, Mississippi where there were many days as a little boy he had walked those long cotton fields in order to get to another family member's house.

He had told me many stories of being afraid of those long dirt roads that he had avoided because of the fear of being caught by the KKK and being lynched in a tree by a rope. He had always told me to stay close to the house. My grandparent used to share a lot of stories with me all of the time and there were a lot of days that we would go for long drives again through the delta.

Living with my grandparents, I had no worries and most of all; I had a sense of security!!

My grandparents had signed me up for school and the school was located in Bolivar County in Shelby, Duncan county line. I knew that I had to go to school every day and that I needed to make go grades. Also while living with my grandparents, there court and Department of Human Services worker had visited our home two days a week in order to see if everything was ok ad that my grandparents were receiving everything services that was available to us.

The workers were really great with us and helped my grandparents a lot. Things were good. After living there in Alligator, Mississippi with my grandparents, the workers had noted that we needed to go back to court to see if my mother was going to get me back. I recall some days when we had gone to court, my mother was there but my stepfather wasn't. I didn't really understand until this day, why my mother had to go to court, but my creepy ass stepfather didn't. my mother wasn't the one abusing me, it was him!

The social workers had explain to me that my mother failed to protect me and that was why she had to go to court, but not my stepfather. My stepfather would be charges at a later date and time. The court date was to determine if I would return back to my mom and I just thought to myself, if I told the truth, then everything would be ok. But it turned out differently than I expect!

There were a lot of days that we went back and forth to court and I had started to feel that I wasn't ever going to go back home to my mother. I had to just deal with it and look at life without her and my brothers!

Grandmother and I had planted vegetables on the side of our house while my grandfather planted things at the back of the house. Living with my grandparents was really exciting. I sit her thinking and smiling as I type.

My grandfather would blast music and shake his head and his bare feet. Lol, my grandfather was so amazing as well as my grandmother. She would sit for hours watching the cars go past while she dipped her Levi Bitter

Garrett Snuff. She would always call me, as I set in my bedroom reading whatever book my grandfather had bought me as he returned from town; she would called me "Pearl, bring me another spit cup! and I did. I brought the spit cup and took the one that she was using and dumped the spit and tissue out in the toilet and had taken it in her bedroom until my grandmother had request for me to bring it back.

Living with my grandparents was always fun and exciting. They had prepared delicious meals and gave me snacks all of the time for being good. My grandfather used to make rock candy and candy that he made from molasses and peanuts. Oh, they were so good! Some of the meals were mostly consist of fish and chicken, along with wild greens that I had to pick from the front of the yard, and hot water cornbread, and sun tea that my grandmother would make by mixing the tea bags with fresh lemons and place in a large pitcher on the front porch for several hours. We had a blast, my grandparents and I.

After living with my grandparents for about a year, the social workers and the court felt that everything was going well, I was doing great in school and was following the rules that my grandparents and workers had given me. The courts had allowed my mother and my brothers to visits us and that I could have about four hours with them and that if everything went well, then I was able to visit at their home, back down in Glen Allen, Mississippi.

My grandparents got the house ready for my mother and brother's visit with us and that I remember being excited with anticipation for their visit. Time was going by so fast and there wasn't one visit from my mother and brothers. I had started to think and feel that my mother and brothers didn't love or want me anymore!!!

I remember sitting for days at time thinking and wondering why they had not came for the visit like the court and the social worker had stated. After so many days and weeks had past, I just remember thinking to myself that I didn't care about anything anymore and as a child I didn't know what to think. I had started to ask God to give me the strength to help me get through this and that the thought of dying had become my only option. I had thought to myself, that I just didn't want to hurt anyone ever again!

My mother and brother never came for a visit for a while and that there we still thing that she may have had to have done, we just didn't know what they were. In my mind, I thought that my damn stepfather may have prevented my mother from coming to see me!

I went on with my day as nothing had ever happened or the thought that my mother and brothers were coming for a visit. Living with my grandparent there in Alligator, Mississippi had become fun and exciting. There were more days that we had gone for long drives through the Mississippi Delta and then back home again.

There were days that we had just sat around the house in our bedrooms just alone taking naps and just watching the television.

My grandparents were extremely caring for me and I thank God that I had them.

Notes

Notes

Chapter 16: Reunited with my Mother and brothers…..

I had attended class on a regular basis instead of going to all of the court dates against my stepfather, even though he never showed up at the court. I just didn't think about it anymore and that nothing after that mattered. I thought about my family's visit and didn't know when it would have ever taken place.

There were so many days that I had come home from school and stayed in my bedroom. The longing for my family had stated to fade away fast and that they went on with their lives without me. They didn't care anymore!

I remember days while being in my bedroom, I I laid thinking and that the thoughts in my head has started to drive me crazy and my grandmother would always tell me to get my behind up and stop thinking so much and go outside and play with the children across the field in the trailer park. I listened to her and went walking outside until I came across some girls that I had gone to school with.

I introduced myself to them and started to be friends with them. I guess that what I had needed in order to stop focusing on my mother and brothers.

It was on a Friday evening, I was walking home from one of the girl's home so that I can eat dinner and as I was walking, I had this strange feeling that had come over me. I picked up my pace so that I could get home and all of a sudden I noticed this strange looking car that was parked across from the old slave shake that was next to our home.

I didn't know whose car it was and maybe it was my mother and brothers, so I had walked a little faster to see. As I had approached the car, a man sat up and looked at me. OH NO!!!! NOOO, I had thought to myself, it was him. My stepfather. Go, help me. No…I turned as fast as I could to get back to our home and as I reached the grass of our front yard, my stepfather had started up his car and headed right at me. I ran and I ran until I reached the front door and snatched it open and ran into my bedroom, hid under my bed without making any noise. I lay there until I cried myself asleep!

I can't recall what time it was when I heard my grandmother calling for me, she fussed and fussed at me because I didn't know that she had called me. It was dark and I was afraid to come out from under my bed. But she told me that she was going to put me on punishment if I didn't come see what she had wanted. I went in to bedroom to see what she had wanted and she had asked me if I was hungry. I replied, "No Mamma", and asked if I could be excused. She went on to ask me if I was ok and said, 'Yes Mamma".

My grandmother had told me that I was excused from dinner and then I went back to my bedroom as if nothing was wrong. I closed the door of my bedroom shielding it with the recliner that was in the far left corner of the room and peeped out of the window to see if my stepfather was still out there or was it all in my mind.

There was no one out there and that maybe I had panic. He wasn't there anymore. But in my mind I still thought to myself that I wasn't going back out there anymore until the court had put him away for good!

Several weeks had gone past when it would be the day that my mother and brothers would finally come for a visit with us, but in my mind I didn't feel like I belonged I thought that everyone hate me and that I remember feeling like an odd ball, so, I went back in my bedroom and stayed there for the whole visit that they were there.

I remember crying there in my bedroom alone and that no one never came looking for me as if I had never been there in the first place.

My mother and brothers had left the next day back to Glen Allen, Mississippi and that my mother just told me to be good she would see me later. Then they were gone!

It was a few months later when the time had arrived before I would have seen them again, one reason was due to the court situation and the second was because of the drive that my mother would have taken to get from Glen Allen, Mississippi to Alligator, Mississippi for my mother with three little boys....

I guess I should have been satisfied with the visit that I did get and not worry about anything at all. I think at that point in my life, I thought that I wasn't worthy of my families love and that they didn't owe me anything!!

Time had gone by and I didn't think about anything or anyone. I just focused on school and playing with my new friends. There were a lot of days that my grandparents had gone fishing while I was at school and then they would sometimes returned home in the late even or late at night. I knew what they had expected of me, therefore, all I had done was; done all of my chores, finish my homework, and get something to eat and stay in the house.

That wasn't too hard for any kid my age. I just remembered that the main thing that I was ever told to do was follow directions and rules!!!

As I continued to do what was asked of me, my grandparents felt that I was responsible enough to be at the at by myself while they took care of bills or went to visit relatives up town. I had, at least I thought in my mind that I was just like any other young responsible kid and that I was ok with being at the house by myself.

Three months had gone by since I had seen my mother and my brothers and it really didn't bother me too much. My grandparents had taken good care of me and that was all that matter. There were so many days when I had walked across the field to play with the other children in the small town. I had a lot of fun being there at the house alone and that I wasn't afraid anymore!

It was around mid-March when I had started to walk up to the corner gas station there in Alligator, Mississippi all by myself and it wasn't any problem for me. It wasn't any difference from any other walk that I had taken. The same route, the same journey down the long rocky graveled road; that when the sun rays beat down on the road, it cast a shiny glow of each stone as I had taken every step.

This particular day, I remembered feeling strange, I can't really recall what had come over me, but I knew that something wasn't right. I recall that I had started to pick up my pace as I walked so that I could get back to the house. As I approached the entrance of the graveled rocky road that leads to our house, I pretended as if I didn't notice him and hurried up to the house. Felt my feet walking really fast as if I was about to start running.

I notice the lights of his car getting closer, my heart started to beat faster. Please God, get me home… Tears ran down my face and I was afraid that he was going to kill me, because of the secret that I had told. Every breath that I had taken had become deeper and deeper, as if I was in a marathon race. I felt myself getting light headed and I stopped, my hand was on the knob of the front door, I opened it without thinking and I was inside of the house.

I remember telling my grandparents that I had seen my stepfather and they just thought it was all in my mind. Why would he drive al that way that night and he knew that he would get in trouble.

They had told me that my mind was running away from me again and that I should have gone to bed and not think about it or him anymore, because I was safe!

May it was all in my mind, but just in case, I put the old recliner behind my bedroom door and made sure that the window in my room was completely shout and locked. I then went into the kitchen to get the biggest butcher knife that my grandparents had and returned back to my bedroom and got my pillow and hid under my bed wrapped in my blanket. Lying under the bed felt comforting to me and I felt safe, because if he was looking in, then he couldn't see me.

I had started to watch everything around me and made sure that I paid attention to everything and everyone around me. I had started to avoid going outside to play with the kids across the field and that my grandparent had made me start going back outside again because I shouldn't be afraid of nothing, but for me, I was afraid of something and someone!!

I had no other choice but to go back outside and lay as if there was nothing in the world to be afraid of. Every step that I had taken was as if a turtle had beaten me to the end of the road. I watched every corner of each direction and behind me as I went to play. Every blue car frightened me and that when I noticed one approaching or passing me, I had ran to the first set of trees in order to hide.

I became so afraid that the outside world had turned on me, in my mind; it felt as if I was over in Iraq trying to dodge every bullet, every step that I had taken, every planted bomb on the ground in order to play with the children across the street and back home before dinner.

My ant from back home n Lansing, Michigan had called my grandparents and told them that she was sending my youngest aunt, the baby sister of my mother; to live with us and that she wanted to come visit.

In my mind, I was over joyed with excitement but at the same time, I was afraid of what they had thoughts about me. I felt as everyone had blamed me for breaking and destroying the family, and they HATED ME!!!!

My aunt Connie is a year older that myself and she along with another cousin who is older than the both of us, were my best friends.

We all were really close to each other's and that I knew when my aunt Connie had come to live with us, she would protect me and play with me.

Notes

Notes

Chapter 17: Aunt Connie is coming....

It was right after school had let out for the summer when my aunt Connie had moved with us in Alligator, Mississippi in the middle of June.

When she arrived with my other aunt and uncles from Lansing, Michigan, I recall that they all had given me the biggest hug ever and that I was really happy when they came. I loved my aunt Bonnie and that she had always been there for me. I remember as I set hear writing now, I just wanted to get to my aunt and live with her back home in Michigan. My aunt Bonnie had taken real good care of her children, especially her daughters. They had the most beautiful hair, cleanest brown caramel skin, and were always dress to kill. They always had the first new children's toys that had come out back then like the "Green Machine Big-Wheel" and the "Sit and Spin" toy…they had it all!!!

I was really excited when my aunt and uncles had come for that visit when they had brought my aunt Connie to live with us.

My aunt and uncles had stayed for a whole week and then my mother and brothers had come for a visit as well as we had started to go visit my mother and brothers down in Glen Allen, Mississippi. The social worker felt that it was ok for me to have visits there and that everything seemed ok, well at least they had thought.

The days that my aunt Connie was there living with us, I felt a since of trust and security that she would let anything happen to me. On the days that we had visited my mother, my stepfather would leave and go up town somewhere or to the grocery store that my mother and him had still. Nothing had changed, only the fact that everyone in town looked at me crazy as if they had seen my photo on a poster that indicated that I was a wanted fugitive or something!

I felt very uncomfortable, so on the days that we had visited my mother, I tried to stay home in Alligator. But it was too far for my grandparents to leave me unattended for that period of time. Therefore, that meant that I had no other choice but to go and on the days that we had gone, I just sat in the hot car for most of the visit. I was afraid that my stepfather would try to do something to me or kill me for telling on him!

Once we had arrived back home in Alligator, I hurried out of the car so that I could get in the house, at that point in my life I remembered that I didn't want to be around anyone and that I had spent a lot of my days either in my closet or under my bed. I didn't want anyone to be around me and then I wouldn't have to hurt anyone else again.

My aunt Connie had helped me to get over my feelings and being afraid, by talking with me and telling me that I didn't have to live my life in fear. To come from under the bed when she discovered that I was hiding again, but the fear of my stepfather was worse than believing anything that she had ever told me.

I used to tell her that I was so afraid and that I didn't want to like that anymore. Just let me be and I just felt really safe under the bed or in the closet. Please just let me be, but my aunt Connie just kept on trying to get me to be safe and not be afraid anymore. She just wanted me to come out and play with her. After a while I slowly came out for a few minutes to eat or take a shower, but when my aunt Connie had told my grandfather what was going on with me, he told me to get my behind from under the bed and that if my stepfather had ever tried to hurt me again, then he would shout him dead like the dog he was!!!!!!

I had believed in my grandfather and that I trusted him. I came out from under the bed and had started to continue on with life as if nothing had ever happened.

There were a lot of days that my aunt and I had gone across the field to play with the other kids and that I remember having a whole lot of fun with my aunt Connie and the other kids. There was a smile on my face again and the thought of my stepfather coming to kill me or do something to me had slowly started to fade away…..

Many days had gone by and there were not one any signs of my stepfather and life was ok then, but in my mind I till felt a little scared!!!

Notes

Notes

Chapter 18: My Stepfather is back!!!!

There, in the small town, everyone was getting ready for a fest and that all I knew was that I didn't want to see no alligators and if I had, I would be the first to run…I just remembered that I had always looked around to make sure that I didn't walk up on no alligator around there. My aunt Connie was never afraid of anything; she had left many days without worrying about a stupid alligator or anything.

As everyone was enjoying them in town, I walked home and that I wasn't afraid. I walked through the town and then ran across the highway, the walked down the long gravel rocky road to get to our house.

There he was, parked again at the base of the graveled rocky road, my feet froze and I had nowhere to run. What was I going to do I thought to myself.

My heart was beating fast and I thought I was going to die right there.

I ran to get to the house; he jumped out of the car and grabbed me as I reached the door. My heart was racing, all could do was beg him to stop, please don't!!!

He had whispered in my ears, "You're going to be mines and nobody will ever stop me, No one!!!

Because if anyone had gotten in his way, then, he stated that he would kill them. "I will kill your aunt Connie, your grandma, and your grandfather!!!"

He threw me down, and walked away. All I remember doing was sit there and scream....scream as loud as I could, because I became so pist! I knew right then and there that I would never be free from him!!!!

My stepfather was back and this time it was worse. There were several days out of the week when I had noticed that blue four door

Dotson parked at the corner of the road and that no matter who I thought I could tell, they just had told me that it was all in my mind! No matter what I had done or said, no one ever listened to me.

In my mind, I thought about poising him and then I'll be free of him. But how would I do that and be free forever?

I knew that my thoughts were wrong, but I was desperate and that I just wanted to be free from him!

I surrendered and whatever happened, just happened and I didn't care anymore! It was in God's hands!

It was during one late afternoon, my grandparents had gone to Clarksdale, Mississippi while my aunt Corrine had gone across the street to play with the other children. I was home alone and remembered that I had to finish doing my chores before my grandparents returned home. I went back into the house after picking some green tomatoes out of my grandparent's garden, so that I could finish my chores.

I washed the lunch dishes and set the table for diner, and put all of the dirty clothes in the clothe hamper. After completing everything that I had to do, I recall turning the shower on in order to take a bath so that I could go outside to play with my aunt Connie and the other kids across the street.

I went in to take my shower, and then afterwards into my bedroom so that I could get dress, until I heard noise. I thought it was my aunt Connie but she never replied or addressed herself. So I didn't think of anything after that, my mind was lost and I ready to be free of the fear....

The following weeks, I had blank that blue car out of my mind and that whatever happened just happened to me. I didn't care anymore!

It was around 6:00 p.m. that evening when I was home all alone, as I walked from the kitchen to the bedroom to get my clothes and towels in order to take my bath, I turn because I had felt like I had heard a noise or something, but I didn't see anything. It was like every step that I had taken, I had heard the noise again, but I wasn't sure where it was coming from and that I just thought that it was all in my mind. The door was locked and I knew that my aunt was across the street with the other children, so I was in the house alone.

I went to take my shower and then right after, I had gone in my bedroom to get dress and that when I had heard the noise again. As I went to see what the noise was; I open my bedroom door and that was when I saw his hairy black scary face. It was my stepfather!

Fear had consumed me and I was paralyzed, unable to move. I panic and ran, clutching the towel that was around me, I ran in order to get away from him. He was faster than I was and then he grabbed me, chocked me by the neck, and told me to shut the hell up!

I panic, unable to breath, my heart danced with every breath that I had taken.

"I cried and beg him, "Please don't hurt me?"

He threw me on the bedroom floor and I tried to run out of my bedroom into the living, so that I could get out of the house. But he was too damn fast and I couldn't do anything. I bit him on his left arm and the only room that I could have gone in was that of my grandfathers'.

I just wanted to get away from him and I didn't think about getting in trouble from my grandfather. I ran in my grandfather's room as fast I could, but he still was able to catch me. All I could do was think to myself, "Why me? I was only 14 years of age and why wouldn't he leave me alone!"

As he grabbed me, we fell to the floor with him landing on top of me.
"Get off of me, you bastard!" "Get off!"

I screamed as loud as I could, but no one heard me. He started to take the towel of me, placing his hand on my thigh, while holding my neck with the other hand so that every time that I moved, it was more difficult for me to breathe.

He preceded licking me on my face, then on my chest, until his mouth was on my breast. I tried kicking and kicking, but it wasn't any use, he was too strong. I grew tired from struggling with him, my body became tired and he over powered me like a fight between an lion and his prey, surrendering until death!!!. I laid there limp, unable to get my thoughts together.

I surrendered, because he was inside of me and I was exhausted. He took my left leg and placed it over his right shoulder as he placed his right hand on my breast as he continued kissing and licking me all over. I turned my head as he continued inside. The pain was unbearable. I felt as if my whole inside was being ripped apart. I fought and I fought, screaming and begging him to stop!!!

He grew anger because I fought against his sexual delivery. He then took my other leg, throwing it on the right shoulder again, having all control over my strength. I was powerless. His penis crushed my ovaries down to my pelvic bone.

I couldn't fight any longer, until I gave in, hoping that it wouldn't hurt if I didn't fight anymore.

The pressure from the weight of his body, had taken over me and I laid there crying. He placed his hand over my mouth as he continued rapping me. I felt a cold fluid running down my behind not realizing that it was the blood from my body. He pushed and pushed until he released himself inside of me. He kissed me and whispered, "You will always be mines, no matter what, and you better remember that!!!"

He continued kissing me all over, as I closed my eyes, when I opened them, he was gone.

I lay there quietly, unable to think. My head started hurting and spinning from fear of what had just taken place. I reached for my bath towel, so that I could get up and recovery myself. As I sat up, there on the white carpet of my grandfather's room, blood, God, blood everywhere. "OMG, I knew that I was really going to be in trouble". How could I have explained that blood on the white carpet!!!!

As tears flowed down my eyes and panic set in,

I remembered taking in the deepest breathe that I ever had, as if it was my last. Collected myself and sat up. My body hurt it so bad that I thought that I had gotten hit by a semi-truck.

I took in another deep breathe and picked myself off of the floor, looked around to see how much blood there was, with the hopes that I could have taken a cold or hot water to clean it up. But discovering that the blood was in a bigger placed than I had previously thought, I knew that I was in trouble.

I rushed to the bathroom and blood continued to run don my legs, I made it to the bathroom, turned on the hot water, to get in.

Washed my body until I scrubbed some skin off parts of my body, then my face with soap until I thought that I had scrubbed of his presence off of every inch off of my body.

My skin was burning from the pot scrapper that I had used to take a bathe instead of using it to wash the dishes. Then threw it I the trash after taking the bath. I jumped out and put my clothes on so that I could get some water in a bucket to clean up the blood. The hot water wasn't working, I remember becoming scared that I was going to get in trouble and then I would be sent back to the home for children in Greenville, Mississippi.

So, I grabbed and put on gloves and grabbed the gallon of bleach, poured it in the bucket water and scrubbed the white carpet until the blood was slowly fading away. I remember that I had gone through half of the bottle of the bleach and several buckets of water until the blood was all gone, then took the vacuum cleaner to help dry the carpet before my grandparents returned. Afterwards, I washed my hands with bleach, and then went back to my bedroom and hid in my closet where I stayed until it was time to go to bed.

But once my grandparents returned, my grandfather never realized the truth behind the wet carpet. I lied and told him that I spilled my cup of fruit punch on the carpet and I would take whatever punishment that he had given me, but my grandfather as grateful as he had always been towards me, just told me it would be alight. I hugged him good night and then pretended that I was going to lie in my bed, but once everyone had gone to bed, my shelter, and bed was the closet where I stayed most of my days there until we had to go visit, to court, or when the social worker arrived. The closet was m security blanket and that no one could see the ugliness inside, outside, and all over me. I wanted to disappear.....!!!!!

My thoughts were overwhelming and the thought of death consumed me even more! I felt so dead inside and the only thing that kept me alive was the sound of my beating heart!!!!!

My thoughts, my mind had gone mad, as the hot steaming baths became my blanket, as the sheet of my bed became my shield, the closet had become my shelter, the Dial bar of soap replaced the scent of semen, while the scrapping pad that was used to scrap food off of the black heavy metal skillets was used to scrap his touch off of my flesh, and the material of any clothing protected my skin from being seen by others.

My life was no more!!!!!

Notes

Notes

POEMS FROM MY HEART

<u>Night Terrors come at night!!!</u>

Night visions in my mind as I slept,

I try to get myself all prep for the fight

Prep to run, as the night terrors tries so hard to kill me

This vision seems all too real

I was a helpless little girl

With my innocence stolen,

My world all so shattered,

I ask God, to give me strength,

As every night was a fight to survive!

Not knowing if I was going to live or die,

Memories of those wicked hands, raping me inside

Hands with long sharp nails as they place and forced them inside

In and out, in and out,

All I could do was scream and shout!!!

God, pleasc take these evil dreams out of my mind,

As these Nights vision in my mind robs my soul….

As I lay there in that place and time,

My thoughts race to find the strength to survive

As I lay there with my eyes close tight,

Tears rolled down the side of my face,

As they stains my pillow,

I held my breath

As my body limped like a weeping willow…..

The night terrors of my childhood visions,

Hunts my mind throughout the day

Allowing my mind to stray…

The night images of my painful past,

Robs me when they come at night,

I ask God for strength to help through this fight!!!!

Notes

Why Me!!!!

I often wondered, Why Me!

Why I was chosen to suffer abuse

By you,

Why I was the one that you had to wake up, twist, and bend, until you were in…

Why me, I never knew why,

As I lay down many nights and cried,

I had no one to turn to,

No one by my side……

All alone, in the darkness of my mind,

I grew mad and angry, until I was dead inside.

I often, wondered why,

What went through your sick mind!!

What was it about me?

That I had to be....

You stole the innocence of my childhood,

My teenage years,

As your sickness plaque me with fears!!!!

Like a robber in the dark,

You had no care, nor a heart.....

As I grew older,

I never knew why,

Because you had died!!!!

Notes

Notes

Notes

Notes

Notes

Notes

Copyright © 2013 Pearl Lilly

All rights reserved.

ISBN-13: 978-1481948449

pearllilly06@yahoo.com

Other Titles.........

"Lost Soul of a Child"

"Surviving It All!!!!"

"Raising Hell!!"

"Armored Pearls....."

and ....

"God, Give Me Strength!!!!!"

Copyright © 2013 Pearl Lilly

All rights reserved.

ISBN-13: 978-1481948449

pearllilly06@yahoo.com

Thank you for allowing me to

share my journey…….

Pearl Lilly

Made in the USA
Columbia, SC
05 November 2024